D1242914

On the Map

Reading Maps

Cynthia Kennedy Henzel

ABDO
Publishing Company

visit us at
www.abdopublishing.com

Published by ABDO Publishing Company, 8000 West 78th Street, Edina, Minnesota 55439.
Copyright © 2008 by Abdo Consulting Group, Inc. International copyrights reserved in all
countries. No part of this book may be reproduced in any form without written permission from the
publisher. The Checkerboard Library™ is a trademark and logo of ABDO Publishing Company.

Printed in the United States.

Cover Photo: iStockphoto
Interior Photos: Alamy pp. 17, 23; Comstock p. 10; Corbis pp. 5, 8, 13, 18; Getty Images p. 29;
     iStockphoto pp. 7, 12, 14, 19, 24, 25, 27; Library of Congress p. 11; National Park Service
     p. 23; Washington State Department of Transportation p. 15; Woods Hole Research Center p. 9;
     World Book Online Reference © 2007 World Book, Inc. By permission of the publisher.
     www.worldbook.com pp. 20, 21

Series Coordinator: BreAnn Rumsch
Editors: Rochelle Baltzer, BreAnn Rumsch
Art Direction & Cover Design: Neil Klinepier

Library of Congress Cataloging-in-Publication Data

Henzel, Cynthia Kennedy, 1954-
  Reading maps / Cynthia Kennedy Henzel.
      p. cm. -- (On the map)
  Includes bibliographical references and index.
  ISBN 978-1-59928-953-3
  1. Map reading--Juvenile literature. I. Title.

  GA130.H48 2008
  912.01'4--dc22

                           2007029205

Contents

Reading a Map

A map is covered with unfamiliar lines, symbols, and numbers. It looks like secret code! To read a map, you must understand the code that **cartographers** use.

A reference map provides an overview of an area. These maps should have an orientation and a **scale**. Orientation shows direction, and scale shows distance. Some reference maps also have grid systems that make locating places easier. A reference map that shows a large area uses a projection. Projections **distort** the round earth to fit on flat maps.

People use thematic maps to compare places. Since they are not used to locate places, scale and orientation might not be shown. However, projection is still important on a thematic map.

All of this may seem confusing! But once you know the code, reading a map is easy. To begin, it is helpful to understand that all maps have several common elements. These elements are a title, a source, a date, and a legend.

The more you practice reading maps, the easier they will be to understand. And, you will learn much about the world around you!

A Telling Title

Every map is made for a specific purpose. A map's purpose may be to give an overview of an area, to help you travel, or to compare places.

However, a map is a selective representation. This means that the **cartographer** chose certain elements to put on the map and left other things off. The cartographer lets you know what the map's purpose is with its title.

A map's title should convey two things. First, it should tell you what is represented on the map. For example, is it a city, a country, the world, or the moon?

Second, the title should tell you what type of information is on the map. Does it show roads, changes in deer population, or where kids eat the most potato chips? A map's title will help you choose the right map to find the information you need.

A map title should be noticeable. This map title's large print and scroll background help it stand out.

The Spanish Main

Florida

St. Augustine

Nassau

Bahama
Islands

Havana

Cuba

Atlantic Ocean

Jamaica

Santiago
de Cuba

Port Royale

Santo Domingo

Port au
Prince

Hispaniola

San Juan

Puerto
Rico

St. Martin
Barbuda
Antigua
Guadeloupe

St. Kitts
Montserrat

Dominica

Martini...

Nombre de Dios
Caballos

Gran Granada

Old Providence

Santa Marta

Cartegena

Rio de la
Hacha

Curacao

Coro

Maracaibo

Gibraltar

Puerto Cabello

Borburata

Caraca

St. Lucia
St. Vincent

Bar...

Grenada

Tortuga Margarita

Cumana

Tobag...

Trine...

Caribbean Sea

Nombre de Dios
Puertebello
San Lorenzo

Panama

Pacific Ocean

7

AMERICA

From the Source

Cartographers make maps using information collected by many people from various origins. A map's source tells you who collected the information or drew the map. On a reference map, the source is usually the cartographer or the publisher. On a thematic map, the source is usually the person who collected the information that is on the map.

A map's source is important because it tells you about the map's **accuracy**. Maps are only as accurate as the information used to create them. A map with a **credible** source is more likely to have accurate information.

The source can also alert you to potential **bias** in the map. Imagine you have two maps titled "Best Places to Live in the United States." One is from the Association of American Retired Persons. The other is based on a random survey

We rely on maps to get us from here to there. Bus routes are one reliable source of travel information.

of college students. The two maps will look much different because both groups of people have different ideas about good places to live.

A map's date tells you when the map was made. This is important because places and ideas do not stay the same. New roads are constantly being built. Even countries move their borders! Still, old maps are valuable. They can be compared with new maps to show how landscapes, ideas, or boundaries change. But the newest maps have the most current information.

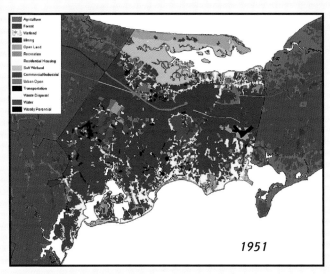

1951

These maps demonstrate the degree to which an area can change in just a few years. The yellow represents population growth in Barnstable, Massachusetts.

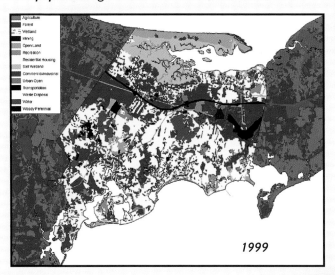

1999

Cracking the Code

You have selected the map you need, and you are satisfied with its source and **accuracy**. Now, it's time to break that map's code!

Cartographers use symbols to illustrate elements on a map. The legend helps you understand what the map's code is communicating. Sometimes the legend is called the key, like the key to a code! The map's legend lists each symbol as well as what it represents on the map.

Reference maps are covered with symbols. Lines may symbolize

A globe is one of the most accurate representations of Earth and the lands upon it.

rivers, roads, or boundaries. Shaded areas may indicate forests, cornfields, or ballparks. Tiny **icons** resembling houses, stars, and trees may highlight other elements.

Thematic maps represent data in cohorts, or groups. A **cartographer** decides how to display the data. Colors, shading, or symbols are used to sort each cohort. Carefully reading the legend helps you correctly interpret the map's information.

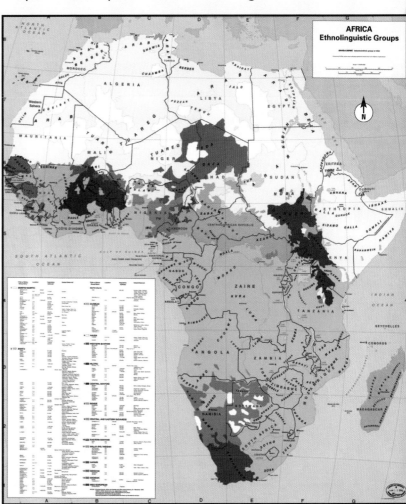

This thematic map uses colors to show the cohorts of languages spoken in Africa.

Which Way Is Up?

A compass rose can be a decorative and beautiful part of a map.

Once you understand your map's code, you need to know which way is up. Orientation involves lining up the directions on the map with the directions in reality. If you don't orient your map, you may end up traveling in the wrong direction!

A north arrow is a map symbol that indicates which way is north. The arrow is often marked with an *N* or the word *North*. It points toward the North Pole. Most maps have north at the top.

Another symbol that shows direction is the compass rose. A compass rose looks like a star or a flower. This is why it is called a rose. It may have four, eight, or more petals. The north petal is always marked.

The four largest petals point to the cardinal directions, which are north, south, east, and west. Smaller petals point to

intermediate directions. These are northeast, northwest, southeast, and southwest.

Once you find which direction is north on your map, you can orient yourself. Use a compass to find where north is. Then, stand facing north. Finally, hold the map in front of you with the compass rose pointing north. You are now oriented with the map. East is to your right, west is to your left, and south is behind you. You are on your way!

How Close or Far?

You are traveling with your map as a guide. How long will it take to reach your destination? To find out, look at the map's **scale**.

Scale reveals the relationship between distance on the map and distance on the earth's surface. Perhaps the distance between San Francisco and Los Angeles is one inch (3 cm) on a world map. But on a state map, the distance between these

From Seattle, Washington, Mount Rainier appears to be close. It even looks near enough to walk to. But don't let your eyes fool you!

Californian cities might be six inches (15 cm). So, how far apart are the two cities? **Scale** helps us find out.

A map's scale may be shown as a word scale, a representative fraction (RF) scale, or a bar scale. A word scale is a written statement such as "one inch equals one mile." Use a ruler to measure one inch on your map. This inch represents one mile (2 km) on the earth's surface. So if your map is 12 inches (30 cm) across, it shows an area 12 miles (19 km) wide.

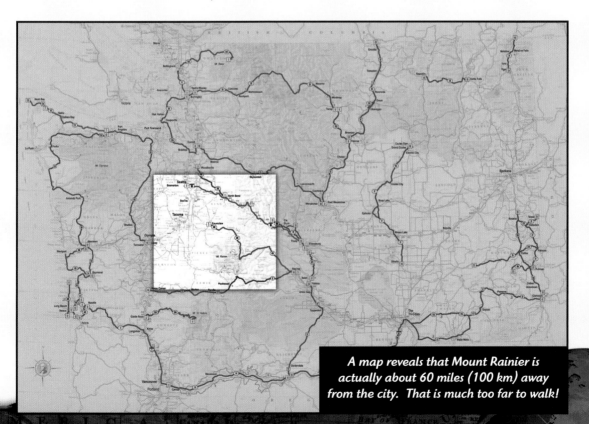

A map reveals that Mount Rainier is actually about 60 miles (100 km) away from the city. That is much too far to walk!

An RF **scale** tells how many units on a map equal a certain number of units on the earth's surface. The RF scale 1:100 means that one inch (3 cm) on the map equals 100 inches (254 cm) on the earth's surface. An RF scale must represent the same units on both sides of the fraction. Since any units can be used, an RF scale is helpful when comparing two different maps.

The third type of scale is a bar scale. A bar scale can be used like a tiny ruler. Usually, the scale looks like a bar drawn on the map. Lines mark various distances along the bar.

In addition to finding distance, a map's scale indicates the level of detail shown on a map. A small-scale map shows a large area with few details. In contrast, a large-scale map shows a smaller area in more detail.

Imagine you are traveling from California to Washington, D.C. A small-scale map can show the entire route. However, it will not give much detail about small roads or things to see along the way.

So, you could use large-**scale** maps of each state to see more detail. The most detailed large-scale map you would need is a city map. It shows only one city, but every street is included.

A globe is useful for locating countries. But, this small-scale map will not help you find your house!

A large-scale map may help you find your favorite restaurant or park. But, it will not tell you how to get across the country!

Downtown New York

Where Are You Now?

Let's say you have chosen a good, up-to-date map of an area. You understand the map's code. And, you know how to determine how far you will travel. Now, where are you on the map? And, where is the place you want to go?

Some maps are posted in one place, such as a mall or a bus stop. Posted maps often mark your location with a star or a colored dot. They may even say, "You Are Here." Now that is easy! However, what if your map does not have this colored dot? Then, you will need a different way to find out where you are.

City map grids often use letters and numbers.

To help you do this, maps often have a grid system. A grid is made of **horizontal** and **vertical** lines that crisscross a map like

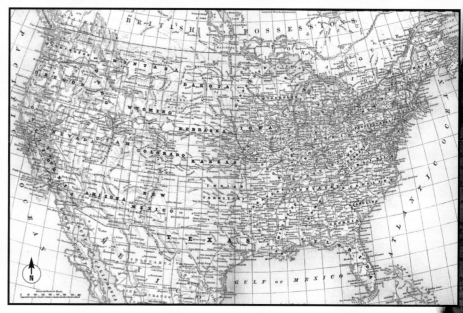

a piece of graph paper. The grid may be drawn on a map, or it may be imaginary. Each grid line is labeled with a letter or a number.

The place where two lines cross on a map is called a coordinate. A coordinate is named after the two crossing lines. With a grid system, the coordinates of countries, towns, roads, or other things are written in an **index**.

For example, an index on a city map might say the coordinates for your school are D6. This means your school is located where the **horizontal** line D crosses the **vertical** line 6. If you follow these vertical and horizontal lines to where they cross on the map, you will find your school.

Latitude and Longitude

Maps of the earth also use a grid system. Lines of latitude extend east and west. The longest line of latitude is halfway between the North Pole and the South Pole. It is called the equator. All other lines of latitude are parallel with the equator. For this reason, they

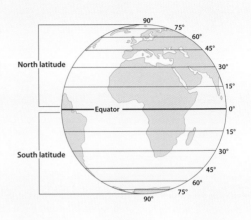

are sometimes called parallels.

The equator divides the earth into two halves called hemispheres. The Northern Hemisphere reaches from the equator to the North Pole. The Southern Hemisphere extends from the equator to the South Pole.

Lines of longitude are drawn from the North Pole to the South Pole. These lines are sometimes called meridians. The line that passes near Greenwich, England, is called the prime meridian. Meridians east of this line are labeled with an *E*. Meridians west of this line are labeled with a *W*. Lines of longitude are not parallel. They become closer together as they near the poles.

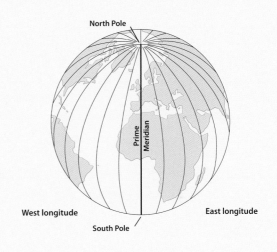

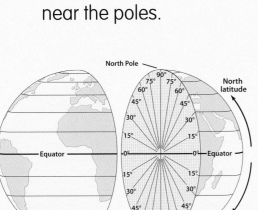

The grid lines in the latitude and longitude system are labeled in degrees. The symbol for degree is (°). The highest degree of longitude lies in the Pacific Ocean at 180° longitude. It is called the international date line. The prime meridian lies at 0° longitude.

The equator is located at 0° latitude. Each degree of latitude is about 69 miles (111 km) wide. The line of latitude that is 69 miles north of the equator is called 1° N latitude. The *N* stands for Northern Hemisphere. The North Pole is 90° N latitude. So, the South Pole is 90° S latitude.

In the latitude and longitude system, coordinates are written with latitude first. The coordinate 38° N, 77° W is read "38 degrees north latitude, 77 degrees west longitude."

To find this coordinate, locate the line of latitude that is 38 degrees north of the equator. Then, follow that line across the map until it crosses the line of longitude that is 77 degrees west of the prime meridian. You should find Washington, D.C., where these lines of latitude and longitude meet.

Degrees of latitude and longitude are not very precise for finding exact locations. Remember, a degree of latitude is about 69 miles wide! Degrees are divided into minutes and seconds to find locations more precisely. Each degree of latitude is divided into 60 minutes. The symbol for minute is ('). Each minute is divided into 60 seconds. The symbol for second is (").

With these more precise measurements, our new location is 38°53'23" N, 77°00'27" W. This is read "38 degrees, 53 minutes, and 23 seconds north latitude and 77 degrees, 0 minutes, and 27 seconds west longitude." Using degrees, minutes, and seconds, you can locate the U.S. Capitol within 100 feet (30 m)!

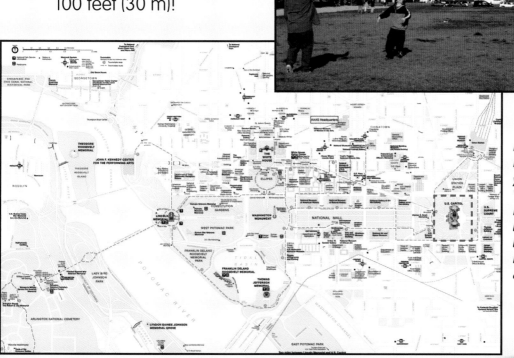

It could take hours to find your way around Washington, D.C. Luckily, latitude and longitude can help you find exact locations!

Wonders of

Niagara Falls, Canada
43°08'15" N, 79°06'42" W

Statue of Liberty, New York
40°68'94" N, 74°04'47" W

Golden Gate Bridge, California
37°81'87" N, 122°47'84" W

Every place on Earth can be identified by coordinates. Are you curious about the coordinates of a certain location? If so, head for a computer! Today, technology allows you to view and explore the planet from your desk. National Map and MapMachine provide interactive maps about different parts of the world. And, Google Earth provides satellite images of any location on Earth, including your house and school!

the World

Colosseum, Italy
41°88'82" N, 12°49'48" E

Pyramids, Egypt
29°97'74" N, 31°13'23" E

Taj Mahal, India
27°17'50" N, 78°04'22" E

Picturing the Planet

A map projection is the way the earth is displayed on a flat surface. The earth is round, like an orange. You cannot flatten an orange peel without tearing or stretching it. **Cartographers** have the same problem when they make a flat map of the round earth. **Distortions** occur in distances, directions, and the shape and size of areas.

A **cylindrical** projection is made by wrapping a piece of paper around a globe. When a light is turned on in the center of the globe, it projects the earth onto the paper. Next, a cartographer traces the projected earth. Then, the paper with the traced globe on it is unrolled to create a map.

The point where the paper touched the globe is the most **accurate**. This means cylindrical projections accurately show areas near the equator. But toward the poles, areas look larger than they really are.

A **conical** projection is made by rolling a piece of paper into a cone and putting it on the earth like a hat. Since the paper touches the earth in the midlatitudes, areas such as North America are most **accurate**. In fact, **conical** projections are often used for maps of the United States.

An **azimuthal** (a-zuh-MUH-thuhl), or planar, projection is made by placing a flat piece of paper on a globe. Since the paper touches the globe in just one place, these maps are only accurate at that one point. So, maps of the poles are often created from azimuthal projections.

Cylindrical Projection

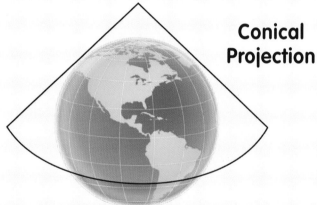

Conical Projection

Azimuthal Projection

27

Today, all types of projections are made mathematically. Each type is used for a specific purpose. The **cylindrical** Mercator projection is one of the most famous projections because it shows true direction. Therefore, it is often used for navigation. However, areas far from the equator are greatly **distorted**. Nevertheless, it was used in classrooms for many years.

Since the 1970s, professional geographers have urged the use of other projections for public maps. They felt students had a **biased** idea of the way the world looks. Many new projections, such as the Robinson projection, were developed to give a more realistic picture of the earth. However, no single projection can **accurately** display the whole earth on a flat map.

Maps are a great way to get information about an area. The title, the source, and the date help you pick an appropriate map. The legend unlocks the code to the information. **Scale**, orientation, and map grids help you find your destination. And, projection shows where map distortion occurs. Now, you understand the secret language of maps. You are ready to explore!

*A map is the perfect tool to help you get out
and become familiar with a new place.*

Glossary

accurate - free of errors.

azimuthal - a projection made from a flat surface. The distance from a point on the projection surface and a point on the earth is expressed as an angle.

bias - a leaning toward one side or point of view.

cartographer - a maker of maps or charts.

conical - shaped like a cone.

credible - believable or reliable.

cylindrical - shaped like a cylinder. A cylinder is a solid figure of two parallel circles bound by a curved surface. A soda can is an example of a cylinder.

distort - to change or misrepresent the normal shape or condition of something.

horizontal - in a side-to-side direction.

icon - a sign, such as a word or a graphic symbol, whose form suggests its meaning.

index - a list of what is in a printed work that tells where to find each item.

scale - the size of a map, a drawing, or a model compared with what it represents. Also, the equally divided line on a map or a chart that indicates this relationship.

vertical - in an up-and-down position.

Web Sites

To learn more about cartography, visit ABDO Publishing Company on the World Wide Web at **www.abdopublishing.com**. Web sites about cartography are featured on our Book Links page. These links are routinely monitored and updated to provide the most current information available.

Index